Songbook

Authors

Lynn M. Brinckmeyer Texas State University, San Marcos, Texas

Amy M. Burns Far Hills Country Day School, Far Hills, New Jersey

Patricia Shehan Campbell University of Washington, Seattle, Washington

Audrey Cardany University of Rhode Island, Kingston, Rhode Island

Shelly Cooper University of Nebraska at Omaha, Omaha, Nebraska

Anne M. Fennell Vista Unified School District, Vista, California

Sanna Longden Clinician/Consultant, Evanston, Illinois

Rochelle G. Mann Fort Lewis College, Durango, Colorado

Nan L. McDonald San Diego State University, San Diego, California

Martina Miranda University of Colorado, Boulder, Colorado

Sandra L. Stauffer Arizona State University, Tempe, Arizona

Phyllis Thomas Lewisville Independent School District, Lewisville, Texas

Charles Tighe Cobb County School District, Atlanta, Georgia

Maribeth Yoder-White Clinician/Consultant, Banner Elk, North Carolina

 in partnership with

Boston, Massachusetts
Chandler, Arizona
Glenview, Illinois
New York, New York

interactive MUSIC powered by Silver Burdett™ with Alfred Music Publishing Co., Inc.

ISBN-13: 978-1-4182-6268-6
ISBN-10: 1-4182-6268-4

4 16

A Ram Sam Sam

Folk Song from Morocco

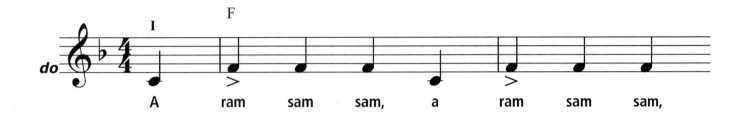

A ram sam sam, a ram sam sam,

Gu - li gu - li gu - li gu - li gu - li ram sam sam.

A ra - fi, a ra - fi,

Gu - li gu - li gu - li gu - li gu - li ram sam sam.

Aguinaldo

Carol from Puerto Rico
English Words courtesy of
CP Language Institute, New York

Aguinaldo

REFRAIN

A la sa - len - de - ra,
Oh, what joy I'm feel - ing,

A la sa - len - de - ra,
Oh, what joy I'm feel - ing,

A la sa - len - de - ra,
Oh, what joy I'm feel - ing

de mi co - ra - zón.
deep with - in my heart.

Ah, eu entrei na roda
(I Came to Try This Game)

Circle Game from Brazil

Ah, eu en - trei na ro - da, pa - ra ver co - mo se dan - ça.
I came to try this game.— I came to see the peo - ple danc - ing.

Ah, eu en - trei na con - tra dan - ça, Ah, eu nao sei dan - çar!
I came here to join the fun, but don't know how to dance!

2nd time: accel. e cresc.

La' vai uma, la' váo du - ás, la' váo três, pe - la ter - cei - ra,
There goes one and there goes two, there goes three, and on the third, There

la' se vai o meu a - mor de va - por p'ra ca - choi - e - ra!
goes my sweet-heart on a steam-boat down the riv - er to the sea.

Al citrón

Latino Nonsense Song from California

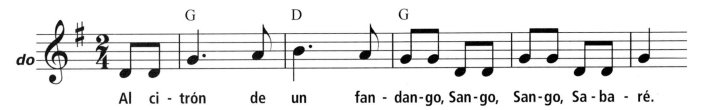

Al ci - trón   de un   fan - dan-go, San-go,   San-go, Sa - ba - ré.

Sa - ba - ré   de   la   ron - de - lla Con su   tri - ki,   tri - ki - trón.

Al tambor
(The Drum Song)

Children's Song from Panama
English Words by Mary Shamrock

Al tam - bor, al tam - bor al tam - bor de la a - le - grí - a,
Won't you play, won't you play, won't you play the *tam-bor - ci - to?*

Yo quie-ro que tú me lle-ves al tam - bor de la a - le - grí - a.
In time with the *tam-bor - ci - to* we en - joy our life to-geth-er.

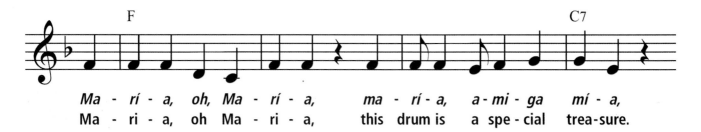

Ma - rí - a, oh, Ma - rí - a, ma - rí - a, a - mi - ga mí - a,
Ma - ri - a, oh Ma - ri - a, this drum is a spe-cial trea-sure.

D.C. al Fine

Yo quie-ro que tú me lle-ves al tam - bor de la a - le - gri - a.
In time with the *tam - bor - ci - to* we en - joy our life to - geth - er.

6

Alabama Gal

Folk Song from Alabama

1. Come through 'na hur - ry,
2. I don't know how, how,
3. I showed you how, how,
4. Ain't I rock can - dy,

Come through 'na hur - ry,
I don't know how, how,
I showed you how, how,
Ain't I rock can - dy,

Come through 'na hur - ry,
I don't know how, how,
I showed you how, how,
Ain't I rock can - dy,

Al - a - bam - a Gal.

Alligator, Crocodile

Words and Music by
Sally K. Albrecht and Jay Althouse

Alligator, Crocodile

great - er than his friend, ___ the croc - o - dile.
smiles, his than fourth big tooth ___ is stick - ing out.

So, if you run in - to ___ an al - li -
So, if you run in - to ___ a croc - o -

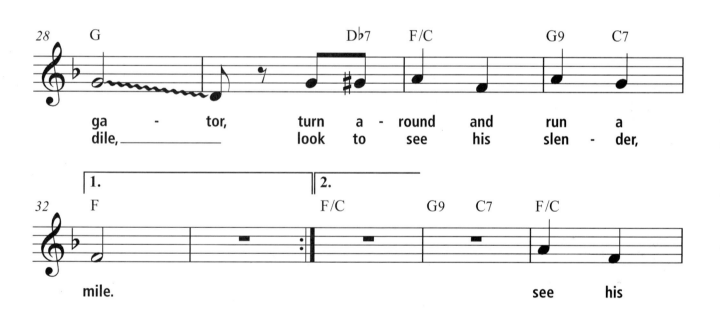

ga - tor, turn a - round and run a
dile, ___ look to see his slen - der,

1.

mile.

2.

see his

slen - der snout. Then run!

9

Ambos a dos
(Go Two by Two)

Folk Song from Latin America
English Words by Aura Kontra

A D

Am - bos a dos, ma - ta - ri - le, ri - le, ri - le,
Go two by two, ma - ta - ri - le, ri - le, ri - le,

D A7 D

Am - bos a dos, ma - ta - ri - le, ri - le, ron.
Go two by two, ma - ta - ri - le, ri - le, ron.

B D G A7 D

1. *Yo ten - go un cas - ti - llo, ma - ta - ri - le, ri - le, ri - le,*
2. *¿Dón - de es - tán las lla - ves? ma - ta - ri - le, ri - le, ri - le,*
1. Come in - to my cas - tle, ma - ta - ri - le, ri - le, ri - le,
2. Where's the key to the door? ma - ta - ri - le, ri - le, ri - le,

D G A7 D A7 D

Yo ten - go un cas - ti - llo, ma - ta - ri - le, ri - le, ron, pon, pon.
¿Dón - de es - tán las lla - ves? ma - ta - ri - le, ri - le, ron, pon, pon.
Come in - to my cas - tle, ma - ta - ri - le, ri - le, ron, pon, pon.
Where's the key to the door? ma - ta - ri - le, ri - le, ron, pon, pon.

10

Ambos a dos
(Go Two by Two)
Recorder Countermelody

Big Rock Candy Mountain

Traditional

1. In the Big Rock Can-dy Moun-tain, There's a land that's fair and bright,
2. In the Big Rock Can-dy Moun-tain, Where the ho-bo nev-er begs,

Where the hand-outs grow on bush-es, And you sleep out ev-'ry night;
And the bull-dogs all are tooth-less, And the hens lay soft-boiled eggs;

Where the box-cars all are emp-ty, And the sun shines ev-'ry day,
All the trees are full of ap-ples, And the barns are full of hay,

Oh, I'm bound to go where there is-n't an-y snow, Where the rain does-n't fall,
There's a lake of stew and___ so-da pop,_ too, You can paddle all a-round

Big Rock Candy Mountain

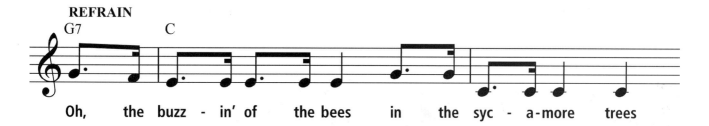

and   the wind does-n't blow, In   the Big   Rock Can - dy Moun-tain.
in   a big   ca - noe, In   the Big   Rock Can - dy Moun-tain.

REFRAIN

Oh,   the buzz - in' of   the bees   in   the syc - a-more   trees

'Round the so - da   wa - ter   foun - tain,   Where the lem - on-ade springs

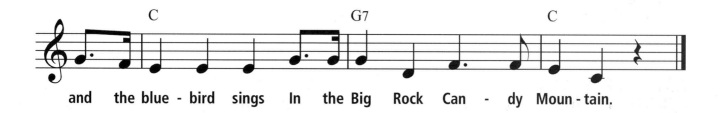

and   the blue - bird sings In   the Big   Rock Can - dy Moun - tain.

Catch the Rhythm

Christine H. Barden

When you hear the rhy-thm,
{ you'll want to move your feet.
{ you'll want to shake your shoul-ders.
{ you'll want to clap your hands.

When you hear the rhy-thm,
{ you'll want to keep the beat.____
{ you'll want to shake your shoul-ders.
{ you'll want to clap your hands.____

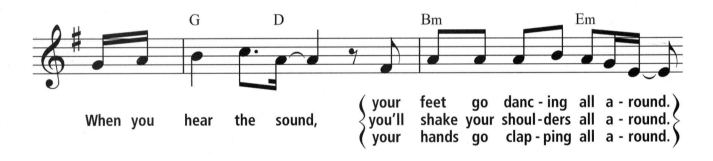

When you hear the sound,
{ your feet go danc-ing all a-round.
{ you'll shake your shoul-ders all a-round.
{ your hands go clap-ping all a-round.

When you hear the sound,
{ you'll go danc-ing all a-round.
{ you'll____ shake them all a-round.
{ you'll be clap-ping all a-round.

Catch the Rhythm

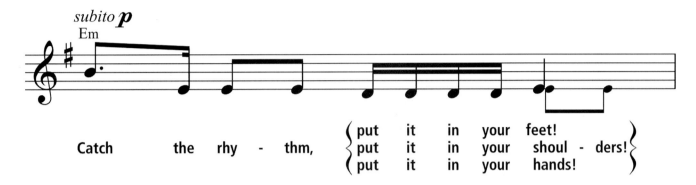

Catch the rhy - thm,
{ put it in your feet!
{ put it in your shoul - ders!
{ put it in your hands!

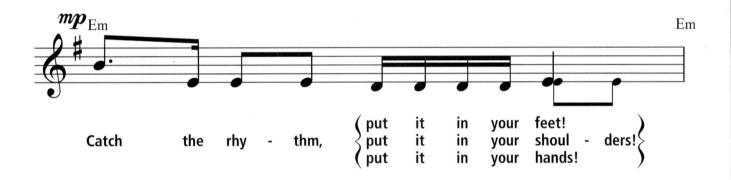

Catch the rhy - thm,
{ put it in your feet!
{ put it in your shoul - ders!
{ put it in your hands!

Catch the rhy - thm,
{ put it in your feet!
{ put it in your shoul - ders!
{ put it in your hands!

Yeah!

Chanukah Games

Music by Judith M. Berman
Words by Rose C. Engle
and Judith M. Berman

5. Whirling, twirling, dreydl, go, on one foot you dance;
Shin says I must put one in and take another chance!
Shin says I must put one in and take another chance!   *Refrain*

Children, Go Where I Send Thee

African American Spiritual

1. Chil-dren, go where I send thee; How shall I send thee?

I will send thee one by one.

Well, one was the lit-tle bit-ty ba - by,___

Wrapped in swad - dling cloth - ing,___

Ly - ing in the man - ger.___

Born, born,___ Born in Beth - le - hem.___

Children, Go Where I Send Thee

2. Children, go where I send thee;
   How shall I send thee?
   I will send thee two by two.
   Well, two was the Paul and Silas,
   One was the little bitty baby,
   Wrapped in swaddling clothing,
   Lying in the manger.
   Born, born,
   Born in Bethlehem.

3. ...I will send thee three by three.
   Well, three was the three men riding,
   Two was the Paul and Silas,...

4. ...I will send thee four by four.
   Well, four was the four come a-knocking at the door,
   Three was the three men riding,...

5. ...I will send thee five by five.
   Well, five was the gospel preachers,
   Four was the four come a-knocking at the door,...

6. ...I will send thee six by six.
   Well, six was the six that couldn't be fixed,
   Five was the gospel preachers,...

7. ...I will send thee seven by seven.
   Well, seven was the seven who went to heaven,
   Six was the six that couldn't be fixed,...

8. ...I will send thee eight by eight.
   Well, eight was the eight who stood by the gate,
   Seven was the seven who went to heaven,...

9. ...I will send thee nine by nine.
   Well, nine was the nine who saw the sign,
   Eight was the eight who stood by the gate,...

10. ...I will send thee ten by ten.
    Well, ten was the Ten Commandments,
    Nine was the nine who saw the sign,...

Chitty Chitty Bang Bang
(from Chitty Chitty Bang Bang)

Words and Music by Richard M. Sherman and Robert B. Sherman
Arranged by Andy Beck

Oh, you pret-ty Chit-ty Bang Bang, Chit-ty Chit-ty Bang Bang,

we love you! And our pret-ty Chit-ty Bang Bang,

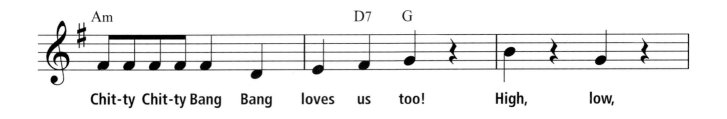

Chit-ty Chit-ty Bang Bang loves us too! High, low,

an - y-where we go, on Chit-ty Chit-ty we de - pend.

Second time to Coda

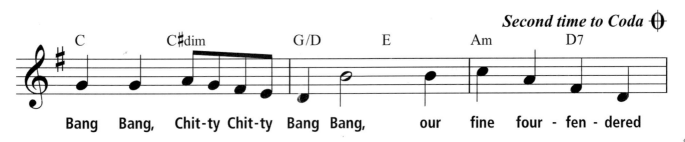

Bang Bang, Chit-ty Chit-ty Bang Bang, our fine four - fen - dered

Chitty Chitty Bang Bang

friend. You're un - cat - e - gor - i - cal; a fuel - burn-ing or - a cle, a

fan - tas - ma - gor - i - cal ma - chine! You're

more than spec - tac - u - lar. To use the ver - nac - u - lar, you're

wiz - ard! You're smash-ing! You're keen!_____

friend. Bang Bang, Chit -ty Chit -ty Bang Bang, our

fine four - fen - dered friend!_____ Bang Bang!

Coffee Grows on White Oak Trees

Folk Song from the United States

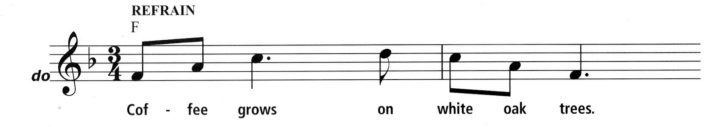

Cof - fee grows on white oak trees.

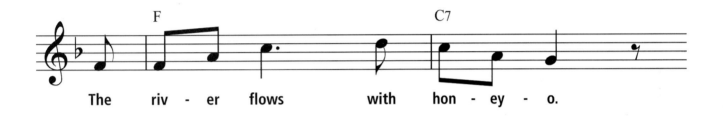

The riv - er flows with hon - ey - o.

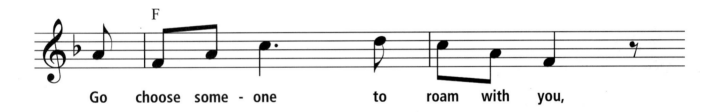

Go choose some - one to roam with you,

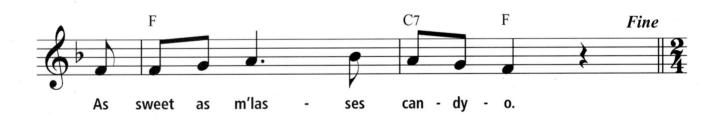

As sweet as m'las - ses can - dy - o.

Coffee Grows on White Oak Trees

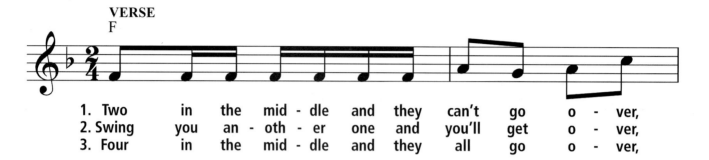

VERSE
F

1. Two in the mid - dle and they can't go o - ver,
2. Swing you an - oth - er one and you'll get o - ver,
3. Four in the mid - dle and they all go o - ver,

F   C7

Two in the mid - dle and they can't go o - ver,
Swing you an - oth - er one and can't you'll get o - ver,
Four in the mid - dle and they all go o - ver,

F

Two in the mid - dle and they can't go o - ver,)
Swing you an - oth - er one and you'll get o - ver,)
Four in the mid - dle and they all go o - ver,)

Bb   C7   F   *D.C. al Fine*

Hel - lo, Su - san Brown.

Creepy Creatures

Words and Music by
Sally K. Albrecht and Jay Althouse

See the creep-y crea-tures lurk - ing all a-bout.

When I see one near me, I just scream and shout!

{ A
{ An

spi - der, a sting - ray, or bum - ble - bee.
earth - worm, a liz - ard, a mouse or bat.

I think they are com - ing af - ter me!
They all seem to know where I am at!

Creep - y, creep - y crea - tures liv - ing in this world.

Creep - y, creep - y crea - tures scar - ing boys and girls. But

Creepy Creatures

wait till you hear what I learned in school: _

each one of them has things that are cool!

See the creep-y crea-tures lurk - ing all a-bout.

When I see one near me, I ____ just scream and shout!

Al - li - ga - tors, croc - o - diles, por - cu - pines that make you smile,

skunks, and snakes, and slim - y old slugs.

Creep-y, creep-y, creep-y, creep-y crea - tures!

Do, Lord

African American Spiritual

Ⓐ **REFRAIN**

Do, Lord, oh do, Lord, oh do re-mem-ber me,

Do, Lord, oh do, Lord, oh do re-mem-ber me.

Do, Lord, oh do, Lord, oh do re-mem-ber me,

rit. last time

Look a - way be - yond___ the blue.

Do, Lord

B **VERSE**

I got a home in glo-ry land that out-shines the sun,

I got a home in glo-ry land that out-shines the sun.

I got a home in glo-ry land that out-shines the sun,

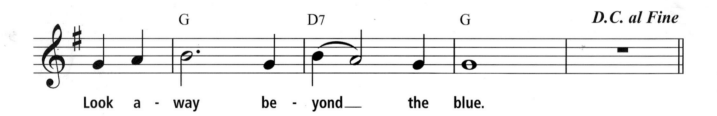

Look a-way be-yond___ the blue.

Don Gato

Folk Song from Mexico

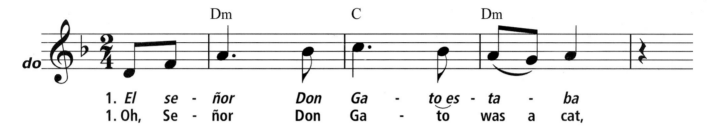

1. *El se - ñor Don Ga - to es - ta - ba*
1. Oh, Se - ñor Don Ga - to was a cat,

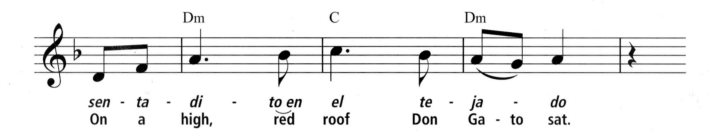

sen - ta - di - to en el te - ja - do
On a high, red roof Don Ga - to sat.

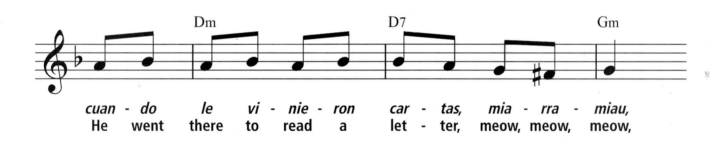

cuan - do le vi - nie - ron car - tas, mia - rra - miau,
He went there to read a let - ter, meow, meow, meow,

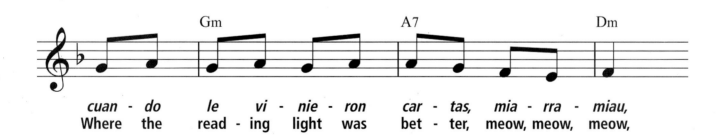

cuan - do le vi - nie - ron car - tas, mia - rra - miau,
Where the read - ing light was bet - ter, meow, meow, meow,

Don Gato

A7   Dm

si   que - rí - a   ser   ca - sa - do.___
'Twas   a   love   note   for   Don   Ga - to!___

2. *Con una gatita blanca,*
   sobrina de un gato pardo,
   que no la había más linda,...
   que no la había más linda,...
   en las casas de aquel barrio.

2. "I adore you!" wrote the lady cat,
   Who was fluffy, white, and nice and fat.
   There was not a sweeter kitty,...
   In the country or the city,...
   And she said she'd wed Don Gato!

3. *Don Gato con la alegría,*
   se ha caído del tejado;
   ha roto siete costillas,...
   ha roto siete costillas,...
   las dos orejas y el rabo.

3. Oh, Don Gato jumped so happily,
   He fell off the roof and broke his knee,
   Broke his ribs and all his whiskers,...
   And his little solar plexus,...
   "¡Ay caramba!" cried Don Gato!

4. *A visitarlo venían,*
   médicos y cirujanos;
   todos dicen que se muere,...
   todos dicen que se muere,...
   que don Gato está muy malo.

4. Then the doctors all came on the run
   Just to see if something could be done,
   And they held a consultation,...
   About how to save their patient,...
   How to save Señor Don Gato!

5. *El gatito ya se ha muerto,*
   ya se ha muerto el buen don Gato;
   a enterrar ya se lo llevan,...
   a enterrar ya se lo llevan,...
   todos los gatos llorando.

5. But in spite of ev'rything they tried,
   Poor Señor Don Gato up and died,
   Oh, it wasn't very merry,...
   Going to the cemetery,...
   For the ending of Don Gato!

6. *Cuando pasaba el entierro,*
   por la plaza del pescado,
   al olor de las sardinas,...
   al olor de las sardinas,...
   don Gato ha resucitado.

6. When the funeral passed the market square,
   Such a smell of fish was in the air,
   Though his burial was slated,...
   He became re-animated!...
   He came back to life, Don Gato!

Don't Let the Wind

Folk Song from St. Helena Island

Don't let the wind, don't let the wind, don't let the wind blow here no more.

Oh, _____ don't let the wind, don't let the wind blow here no more.

El rabel
(The Violin)

Folk Song from Chile
Adapted by Patricia Shehan Campbell with Ana Lucia Frega

El ra - bel pa - ra ser fi - no ha de ser de ver - de pi - no,
The ra - bel it is so fine and it's made of fresh green pine,

la vi - hue - la d(e) du - ra he - bra y el se - dal de mu - la ne - gra,
The vi - hue - la's stur - dy shell you know it holds the strings so well.

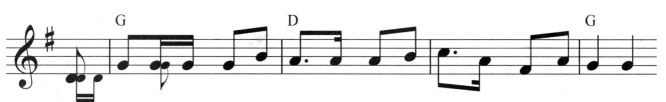

la vi - hue - la d(e) du - ra he - bra y el se - dal de mu - la ne - gra.
The vi - hue - la's stur - dy shell you know it holds the strings so well.

An - da mo - re - ni - ta re - co - je e - se pa - ñue - lo.
Let the girl go there and pick up the hand - ker - chief.

Mi - ra que es de se - da y lo a - rras - tras por el sue - lo.
Silk - en hand - ker - chief: she's drag - ging it on the floor.

Erdö, erdö de magos
(In the Silent Forest)

Folk Song from Hungary
English Words by Jean Sinor

1. Erd - ö, erd - ö de ma - gos a te - te - je.
2. Bu - za ko - zé szállt a da - los pac - sir - ta,
1. In the si - lent for - est sings the lone - ly bird,
2. Through the mist - y tree - top flies the or - phaned lark.

Jaj, de ré - gen le - hul - lot a le - ve - le.
Mert o - da - fenn a sze - meit ki - sír - ta.
Cold winds blow - ing whis - per se - crets nev - er heard,
For - est branch - es creak - ing stiff - ly, bare and stark.

Jaj, de ré - gen le - hul - lot a le - ve - le.
Bú - za - vi - rág, bú - za - ka - lász árn - yá - ban
High a - bove the moon re - flects an i - cy light,
Sad - ly sounds the plain - tive call - ing high a - bove,

Ár - va ma - dár pár - jat ke - re si ben - ne.
Rá - gon - dolt a ré - gi, els ö pár - já - ra.
Sha - dows flee - ing swift - ly through the au - tumn night.
Call - ing in the au - tumn sha - dows for his love.

Four White Horses

Folk Song from the Caribbean

Good Morning

Words and Music by Elizabeth Gilpatrick

Good morn - ing, good morn - ing, I'm glad you're here to - day.

We'll do our work and have some fun and then go on our way.

Great Day

African American Spiritual

The Groundhog Blues

Words and Music by Gayle Giese

The Groundhog Blues

"Whoa!   Back   to   my   log,   I'm   out   of   this   light!" —

'Twas   a   ver - y   sad   thing   that   hog   was   so   meek, —

For   win - ter   roared   for   six____   more   weeks! —

Verse 1 - mf
Verse 2 - f
Verse 3 - ff

Repeat 2 times

I've   got   the   ground-hog   blues; —   it's   win - ter,   it's   cold!

I've   got   the   ground - hog____   blues.   Brrrr!

Happy Feet

Words and Music by Jack Yellen and Milton Ager

1. Hap-py feet! I've got those hap-py feet.
2. Wear-y blues Can't get in-to my shoes.

Give them a low-down beat
Be - cause my shoes re - fuse

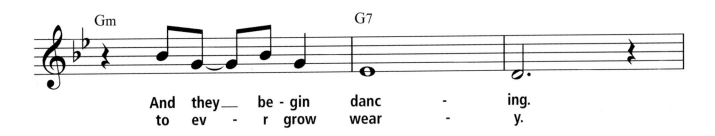

And they__ be-gin danc - ing.
to ev - r grow wear - y.

Happy Feet

I've got those ten lit - tle tap-ping toes

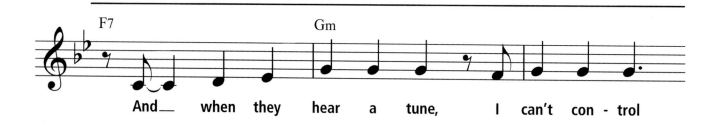

And__ when they hear a tune, I can't con - trol

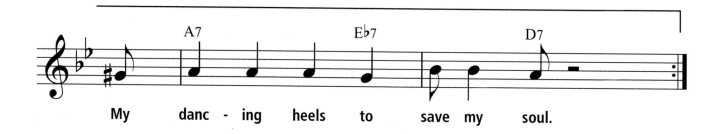

My danc - ing heels to save my soul.

I keep cheerful__ on an ear-ful__ of mu - sic sweet,__

'Cause I've got hap - hap - hap-py__ feet.

Hevenu shalom aleichem
(We Come to Greet You in Peace)

Hebrew Folk Song

Hot Cross Buns

Folk Song from England

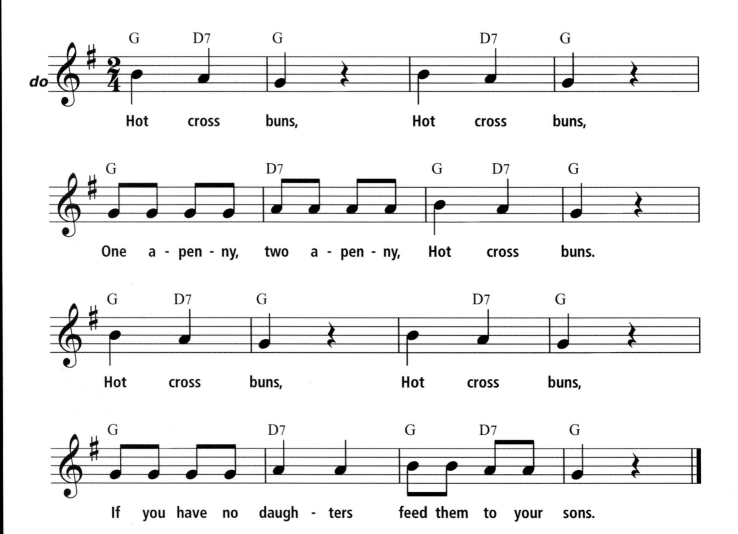

Hush, Hush

African American Spiritual

Hwa yuan li-de young wa wa
(Garden Lullaby)

Music by Chuen-Taur Su
Words by Po-Yang Chou
English Words by Ellen Williams

Mai   mai bay   ge   young wa   wa   jou   dau hwa yuan   lai   kan hwa
Lit - tle sis - ter   with her doll   Walks   a-mong the   gar - den walls.

wa   wa   koo   le   jau   ma   ma   shu   shan siau niau   siau   ha   ha.
"Ma - ma," cries the   ba - by doll.   From   the trees birds   sing their calls.

42

I've Been Working on the Railroad

Work Song from the United States

I've Been Working on the Railroad

Some-one's in the kitch-en with Di - nah,

Some-one's in the kitch-en, I know.

Some-one's in the kitch-en with Di - nah,

Strum-min' on the old ban - jo.

Fee, fie, fid-dle-ee i o, fee, fie, fid-dle-ee i o,

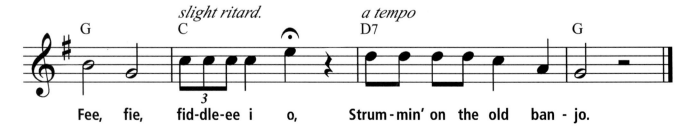

Fee, fie, fid-dle-ee i o, Strum-min' on the old ban - jo.

Ichi-gatsu tsuitachi
(A New Year's Greeting)

Music by Ue Sanemichi
School Song from Japan
Words by Senge Takatomi
English Words Adapted by Katherine S. Bolt

do

To - shi no ha - ji - me no Ta - me - shi to - te
"O - me - de - to go-zai - mas," we will bow and say,

O - wa - ri na - ki yo no Me - de - ta - sa o
"O - me - de - to go-zai - mas," Hap - py New Year's Day.

Mat - su - ta - ke ta - te te Ka - do go - to ni
Let us place our pine branch-es here be - side the door,

I - wo___ kyo___ ko - so Ta - no - shi - ke - re.
And wish our friends and neigh-bors man - y new years more.

If a Tiger Calls

Words and Music by Elizabeth Gilpatrick

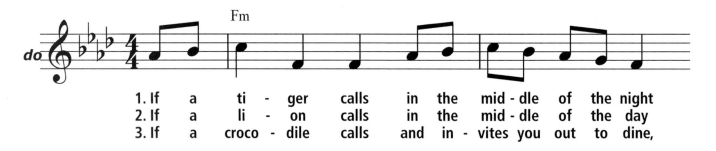

1. If a ti - ger calls in the mid - dle of the night
2. If a li - on calls in the mid - dle of the day
3. If a croco - dile calls and in - vites you out to dine,

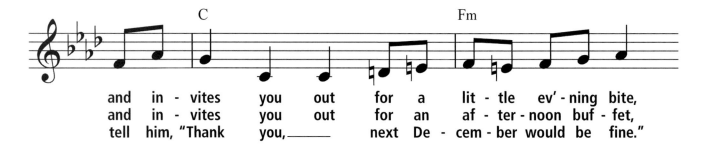

and in - vites you out for a lit - tle ev' - ning bite,
and in - vites you out for an af - ter - noon buf - fet,
tell him, "Thank you,____ next De - cem - ber would be fine."

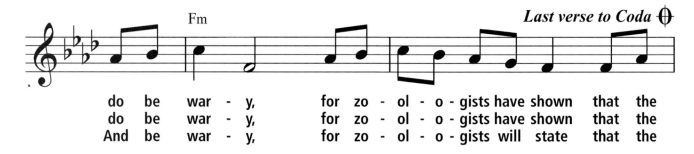

Last verse to Coda

do be war - y, for zo - ol - o - gists have shown that the
do be war - y, for zo - ol - o - gists have shown that the
And be war - y, for zo - ol - o - gists will state that the

ti - ger lies on the phone.
li - on lies on the phone.

If a Tiger Calls

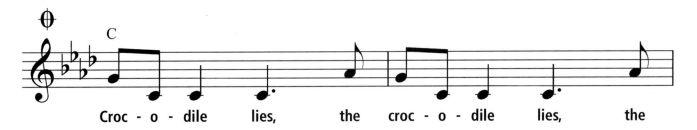

Croc - o - dile   lies,   the   croc - o - dile   lies,   the

croc - o - dile   lies   in   wait!

If I Only Had a Brain
(from The Wizard of Oz)

Music by Harold Arlen
Lyric by E.Y. Harburg
Arranged by Andy Beck

48

If I Only Had a Brain

o - cean's near the shore. I could think of things I nev - er thunk be -

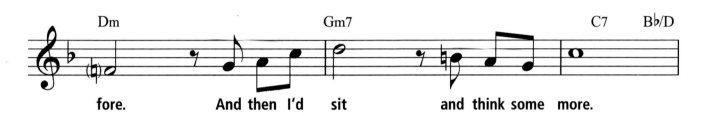

fore. And then I'd sit and think some more.

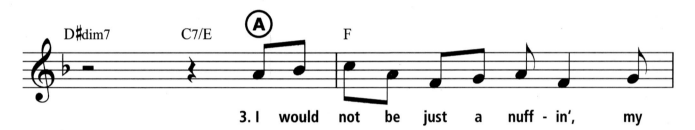

3. I would not be just a nuff - in', my

head all full of stuff-in', my heart all full of pain. And per -

haps I'd de - serve you and be ev - en wor - thy erv you, if I

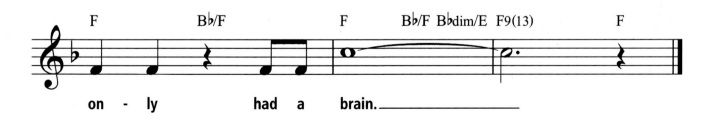

on - ly had a brain.

In the Pumpkin Patch

Words and Music by Elizabeth Gilpatrick

1. When I grew up in the pump - kin__ patch,
2. "Roll a - round lit - tle pump - kin__ in the pump-kin patch;
3. "But__ when the sun is__ sink - ing__ low

I sat in the sun all day.
Oh, tum - ble and turn and sway.
And sha - dows__ steal the light,

I__ grew 'til__ I was__ gold and__ round,
Roll a - round in the gras - es and the weeds and the thatch,
Hur - ry back to your home in the gar - den__ row;

Then I heard a lit - tle sun - beam say:
Oh,__ spin__ and__ roll and play."
Curl__ up__ in your vines so tight."

It's a Beautiful Land We Share

Words and Music by Carmino Ravosa

It's a beau-ti-ful land we share.

A beau-ti-ful land out there.

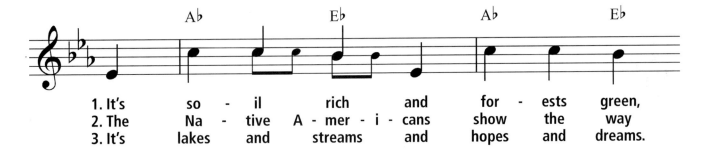

1. It's so - il rich and for - ests green,
2. The Na - tive A - mer - i - cans show the way
3. It's lakes and streams and hopes and dreams.

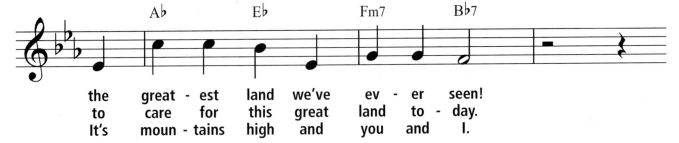

the great - est land we've ev - er seen!
to care for this great land to - day.
It's moun - tains high and you and I.

3rd time to Coda

It's a beau-ti-ful land we share.

It's a Beautiful Land We Share

It's a beau-ti-ful land we share.

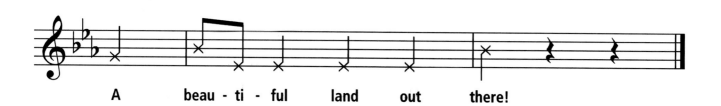

A beau-ti-ful land out there!

Jan ken pon

Collected by Mary Shamrock at the
Nishi Hongwanji Temple Dharma School
English Words by Mary Shamrock

O - na - ka ga su - i - ta - ra goo goo goo,
When you have a hair - cut, scis - sors snip, snip, snip.

Ka - mi - no - ke no - bi ta - ra cho - ki cho - ki cho - ki,
Hun - gry sto - machs of - ten make a grum - ble, grum - ble, grum - ble.

Ho - ko - ri wo ha - ta - i - te pa pa pa,
Wip - ing with a dust rag makes a slap, slap, slap.

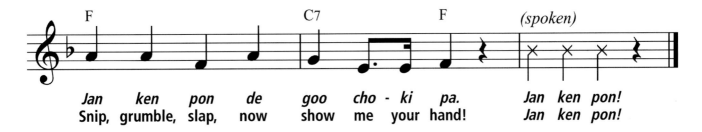

(spoken)

Jan ken pon de goo cho - ki pa. Jan ken pon!
Snip, grumble, slap, now show me your hand! Jan ken pon!

Karangatia ra

Maori Action Song from New Zealand

Keep Your Eyes on the Prize

African American Freedom Song

A VERSE

1. Got my hand on the free - dom plow,
2. We fought jail and vio - lence too,
3. Work all day and work all night,
4. The on - ly chain that a man can stand

Won't give no - thin' for my jour - ney now.
But God's love has seen us through.
Tryin' to gain our civ - il rights.
Is the chain of a hand in hand.

Keep your eyes on the prize. Hold on!

B REFRAIN

Hold on! Hold on!

Keep your eyes on the prize. Hold on!

Knock No More

Words and Music by
Elizabeth Gilpatrick

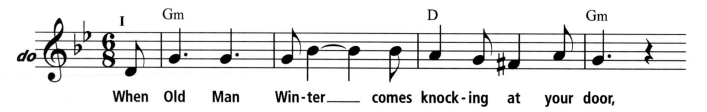

When Old Man Win-ter___ comes knock-ing at your door,

he'll nip your fin-gers___ and freeze you to the core.

Knock! Knock! Can't come in! Knock no more!

La calle ancha
(The Wide Street)

Folk Song from Puerto Rico
English Words by Mary Shamrock

1. La ca - lle an - cha, cha, cha de San Ber - nar - do, do, do
2. Los cua - tro ca - ños, ños, ños dan a - gua her - mo - sa, sa, sa
1. A - long the street wide, wide, wide called San Ber - nar - do, do, do
2. In Za - ra - go - za, za, za They shine and spar - kle, kle, kle

Tie - ne u - na fuen - te, te, te con cua - tro ca - ños, ños, ños.
Pa - ra los ni - ños, ños, ños de Za - ra - go - za, za, za.
There is a foun - tain, tain, tain, from which four streams flow, flow, flow.
For all the chil - dren, dren, dren A gift so sim - ple, ple, ple.

La piñata
(The Piñata)

Folk Song from Mexico
English Words by Alice Firgau

1. En las no - ches de po - sa - das,
2. Con tus o - ji - tos ven - da - dos
1. On po - sa - da nights we have such fun,
2. Put a blind - fold o - ver both your eyes,

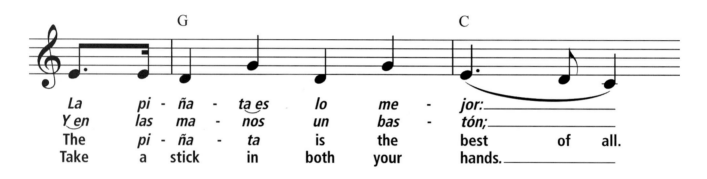

La pi - ña - ta es lo me - jor:
Y en las ma - nos un bas - tón;
The pi - ña - ta is the best of all.
Take a stick in both your hands.

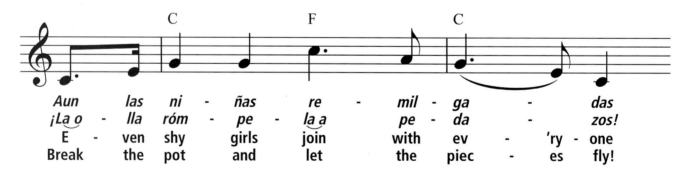

Aun las ni - ñas re - mil - ga - das
¡La o - lla róm - pe - la a pe - da - zos!
E - ven shy girls join with ev - 'ry - one
Break the pot and let the piec - es fly!

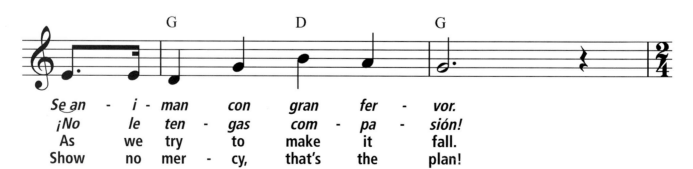

Se an - i - man con gran fer - vor.
¡No le ten - gas com - pa - sión!
As we try to make it fall.
Show no mer - cy, that's the plan!

La piñata

B REFRAIN

Da - le, da - le, da - le, no pier - das el ti - no.
There's the big pi - ña - ta, See if you can whack it,

Mi - de la dis - tan - cia que hay en el ca - mi - no.
Turn and swing, you'll hit it, Hit it hard, you'll crack it.

Que si no le das de un pa - lo te em - pi - no,
And if you don't break it I'll raise you up there like it,

¡Por - que tie - nes au - ra de pu - ro pe - pi - no!
Like a big pi - ña - ta. So you bet - ter strike it!

Li'l Liza Jane

Dance Song from the United States

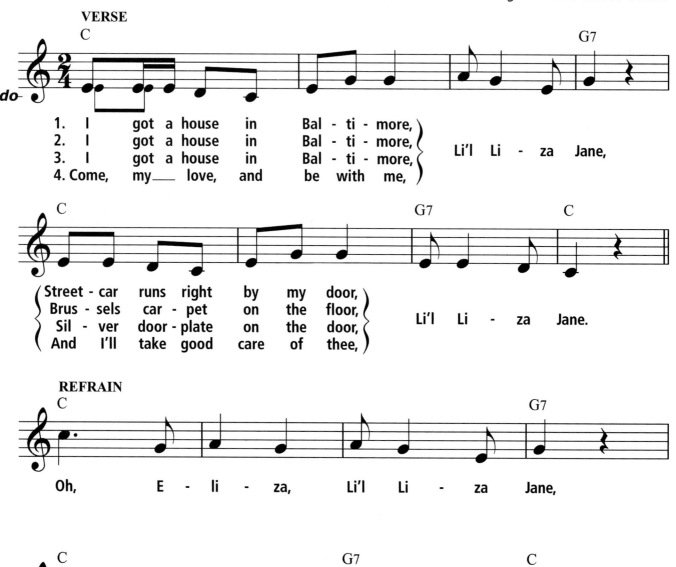

VERSE

1. I got a house in Bal - ti - more,
2. I got a house in Bal - ti - more,
3. I got a house in Bal - ti - more,
4. Come, my love, and be with me,

Li'l Li - za Jane,

Street - car runs right by my door,
Brus - sels car - pet on the floor,
Sil - ver door - plate on the door,
And I'll take good care of thee,

Li'l Li - za Jane.

REFRAIN

Oh, E - li - za, Li'l Li - za Jane,

Oh, E - li - za, Li'l Li - za Jane.

Love Somebody

Folk Song from the United States

Love some-bod-y, yes, I do, Love some-bod-y, yes, I do,

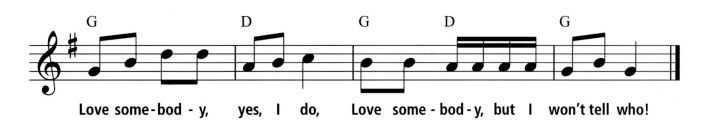

Love some-bod-y, yes, I do, Love some-bod-y, but I won't tell who!

Make New Friends

Traditional Round

Mama Paquita

Carnival Song from Brazil
English Words by Margaret Marks

1. Ma - ma Pa - qui - ta, Ma - ma Pa - qui - ta,
Ma - ma Pa - qui - ta, Ma - ma Pa - qui - ta,

Ma - ma Pa - qui - ta, buy your ba - by a pa - pa - ya,
Ma - ma Pa - qui - ta, says "I have - n't an - y mon - ey

A ripe pa - pa - ya and a ba - na - na,
To buy pa - pa - yas and ripe ba - na - nas,

1. A ripe ba - na - na that your ba - by will en - joy, ma - ma - ma - ma,

2. Let's go to Car - ni - val and dance the night a - way!"

2. Mama Paquita, Mama Paquita,
   Mama Paquita, buy your baby some pajamas,
   Some new pajamas, a yellow blanket,
   A yellow blanket that your baby will enjoy, ma-ma-ma-ma.
   Mama Paquita, Mama Paquita,
   Mama Paquita says, "I haven't any money
   To buy pajamas, a yellow blanket,
   Let's go to Carnival and dance the night away."

Maps and Globes

Words and Music by Carmino Ravosa

Maps and Globes

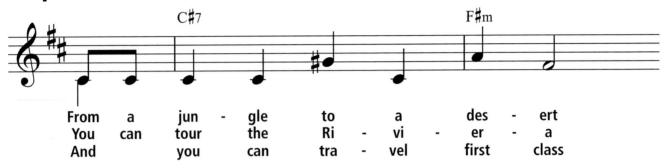

From a jun - gle to a des - ert
You can tour the Ri - vi - er - a
And you can tra - vel first class

G ritard   A7   *D.C. al Fine*

or a - round your own home town.
and be home in own time bed.
and it won't cost you a dime.

Michael Finnigan

Traditional from the United States

do

F
(1., 2., 3., 4.) There was an old man named Mi - chael Fin - ni - gan,

B♭   C
He   had   whis - kers   on   his   chin - ni - gan, The
He   went   fish - ing   with   a   pin - ni - gan, He
Climbed   a   tree   and   barked   his   shin - ni - gan, He
He   grew   fat   and   then   grew   thin - ni - gan, ___

F
wind   came   up   and   blew   them   in   a - gain,
caught   a   fish   but   dropped   it   in   a - gain,
lost   a - bout   a   yard   of   skin - ni - gan,
Then   he   died   and   had   to   be - gin   a - gain,

C7   F
Poor   old   Mi - chael   Fin - ni - gan.   Be - gin   a - gain.

Morning Is Come

Round from England

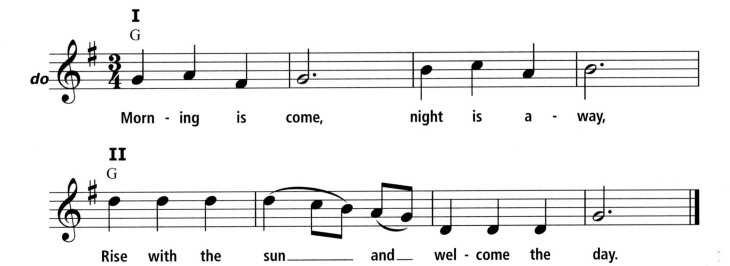

I

Morn - ing is come, night is a - way,

II

Rise with the sun _____ and ___ wel - come the day.

Mübärak
(Happy Birthday)

Persian Birthday Song
As sung by Hooshang Bagheri
English Words by Mary Shamrock

Mù-bä - rak, mù-bä - rak, ta- val - lu-det mù-bä - rak,
Hap-py day, hap-py day, here it is, your hap-py day.

mù-bä - rak, mù-bä - rak, ta-val - lu-det mù-bä - rak.
Hap-py day, hap-py day, here it is, your hap-py day.

La bat shä - di de let khush, chu gul pur khan-deh bä she
May this birth-day bring a year filled with all the best for you;

be-yä sham hä rä fot kun ke sad sâl zen-deh bä she.
As you blow the can-dles out, may your spe - cial wish come true.

Nani wale na hala
(Lovely Hala Trees)

Folk Song from Hawaii
English Words by Alice Firgeu

do—

Na - ni wa - le na_____ ha - la,　　E - a,　　e - a.
Love - ly are the ha - la trees, ___　　E - a,　　e - a.

O_____ Nau - e i - ke ka - i,　　E - a,　　e - a.
Sway-ing by the gen - tle seas.____　　E - a,　　e - a.

Ke_____ o - ni a_____ e - la　　E - a,　　e - a.
Near Ha - e - na ha - las grow,___　　E - a,　　e - a.

Pi - li ma - i Ha - e - na　　E - a,　　e - a.
In Na - u - e breez - es blow.___　　E - a,　　e - a.

Oh, Won't You Sit Down

African American Spiritual

REFRAIN

Oh, won't you sit down? Lord, I can't sit down.

Oh, won't you sit down? Lord, I can't sit down.

Oh, won't you sit down? Lord, I can't sit down.

'Cause I just got to Heav-en, gon-na look a - round.

Oh, Won't You Sit Down

Old Dan Tucker

Folk Song from the United States

1. Old Dan Tuck - er was a might - y man, He
2. Old Dan Tuck - er came to town,

washed his face in the fry - ing pan,
Rid - ing a bil - ly goat, lead - ing a hound;

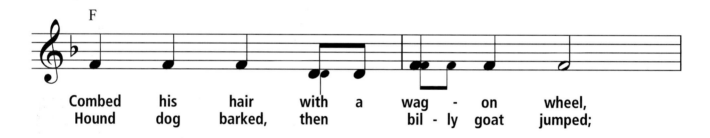

Combed his hair with a wag - on wheel,
Hound dog barked, with then bil - ly goat jumped;

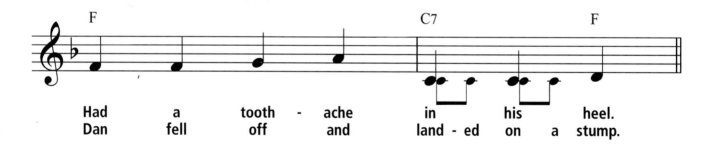

Had a tooth - ache in his heel.
Dan fell off and land - ed on a stump.

Old Dan Tucker

Old House, Tear It Down!

African American Work Song
Collected by John Work

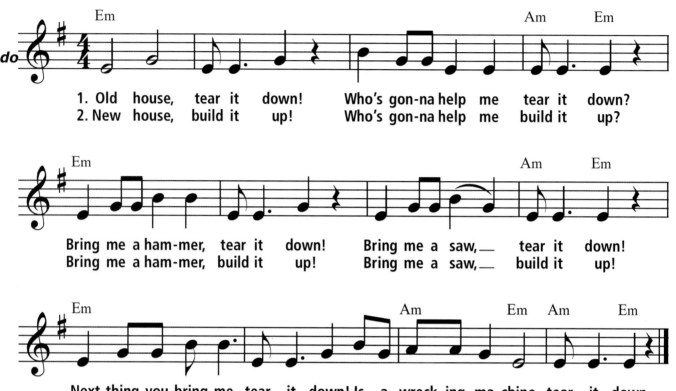

1. Old house, tear it down! Who's gon-na help me tear it down?
2. New house, build it up! Who's gon-na help me build it up?

Bring me a ham-mer, tear it down! Bring me a saw,— tear it down!
Bring me a ham-mer, build it up! Bring me a saw,— build it up!

Next thing you bring me, tear it down! Is a wreck-ing ma-chine, tear it down.
Next thing you bring me, build it up! Is a car - pen-ter man, build it up.

Over the River and Through the Wood

Traditional
Words by Lydia Maria Child

1. O - ver the riv - er and through the wood,
2. O - ver the riv - er and through the wood,

To Grand - fa - ther's house we go;_____
Trot fast,_____ my dap - ple gray!_____

The horse knows the way to car - ry the sleigh
Spring o - ver the ground like a hunt - ing hound,

Through the white and drift - ed snow._____
For this is Thanks - giv - ing Day!_____

Over the River and Through the Wood

O - ver the riv - er and through the wood,
O - ver the riv - er and through the wood,

Oh, how the wind does blow!_____
Now Grand-moth - er's face I spy!_____

It stings the toes and bites the nose
Hur - rah for the fun! Is the pud - ding done?

As o - ver the ground we go.
Hur - rah for the pump - kin pie!

The Planets Chant

Words and Rhythmic Setting by Mary Shamrock

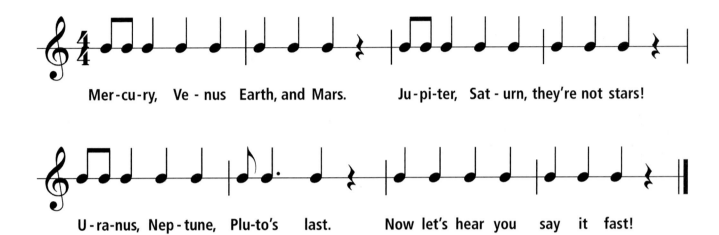

Mer-cu-ry, Ve - nus Earth, and Mars. Ju-pi-ter, Sat - urn, they're not stars!

U - ra-nus, Nep - tune, Plu-to's last. Now let's hear you say it fast!

Pust' 'vsegda budet sonse

(May the Sun Shine Forever)

Music by A. Ostrovsky
Russian Words by L. Oshanin
English Words by Alice Firgau

¡Qué gusto!
(What Pleasure!)

Hispanic Song of the American Southwest
English Words by Ruth De Cesare (adapted)

¡Qué gus - to, qué gus - to, qué gus - to me da,
What pleas - ure, what pleas - ure and joy it gives me

vi - vir en el cam - po con tran - qui - li - dad!
To live in the coun - try, so peace - ful and free!

Yo can - to, yo brin - co a mi li - ber - tad,
I sing and I dance and I jump all a - round,

por - que no hay ti - je - ras de la so - cie - dad.
Ver - y free of the crowds and the noise I once found.

Ragtime Cowboy Joe

Music by Lewis F. Muir and Maurice Abrahams
Words by Grant Clarke

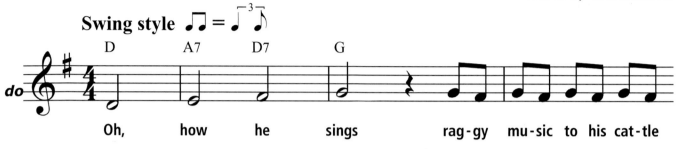

Oh, how he sings rag-gy mu-sic to his cat-tle

as he swings back and forth in his sad - dle

on a horse that is syn - co - pa - ted, gai - ted.

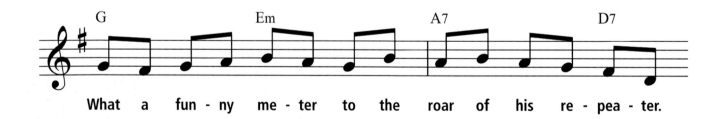

What a fun - ny me - ter to the roar of his re - pea - ter.

Ragtime Cowboy Joe

Sansaw akroma

Game Song from Ghana

Scotland's Burning

Traditional Round
Arranged by Robert W. Smith

Scot - land's burn - ing, Scot - land's burn - ing, look out, look out,

Fire! Fire! Fire! Fire! Pour on wa - ter, pour on wa - ter!

Ostinato

Wa - ter, wa - ter,

Shakin' It Up!

Words and Music by
Sally K. Albrecht and Jay Althouse

Shake, shake, shake.   Shake, shake, shake.   Yeah, we're

(repeat both times)

shak-in' it up!   We're shak-in' it up!

1. Keep-in' a stead - y   beat, you'll find,___
2. We're learn-ing eighth and   quar - ter notes,___

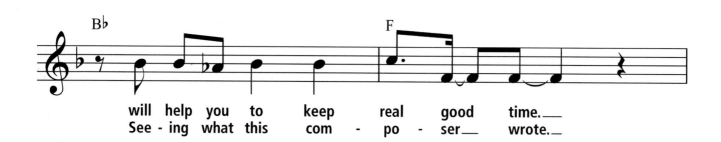

will help you to   keep   real   good   time.___
See - ing what this com - po - ser___ wrote.___

Shakin' It Up!

If you can read it rhyth - mi - c'lly___
Our shak - in' keeps the beat so strong___

You will be strong - er mu - si - c'lly.___
That an - y - one can join a - long.___

Shake, shake, shake. Shake, shake, shake. Yeah, we're

shak - in' it up! We're shak - in' it up!

Silent Night

Music by Franz Gruber
Words by Joseph Mohr

Si - lent night, ho - ly night, All is calm, all is bright

Round yon Vir - gin Mo -ther and child. Ho - ly In -fant so ten - der and mild,

Sleep in heav - en-ly peace, — Sleep — in heav - en-ly peace. —

Soakin' Up the Sunshine

Words and Music by Andy Beck and Brian Fisher

1. Hey, hey, it's a beau-ti-ful day___ and the sun is shin-in' bright.
2. Hey, hey, it's a beau-ti-ful day,___ all the clouds are cum-u-lus.

Hey, hey, it's a beau-ti-ful day___ 'cause the
Hey, hey, it's a beau-ti-ful day___ and the

weath-er is al-right. We're go-in' soak-in' up the sun-
sky is blue for us.

- shine,___ ev'-ry sin-gle ray,

soak-in' up the sun - shine, let's en-joy the day.

Soakin' Up the Sunshine

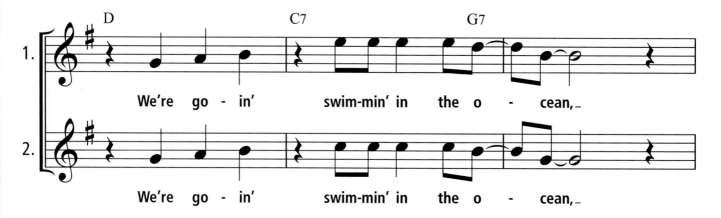

1. We're go - in' swim-min' in the o - cean, _

2. We're go - in' swim-min' in the o - cean, _

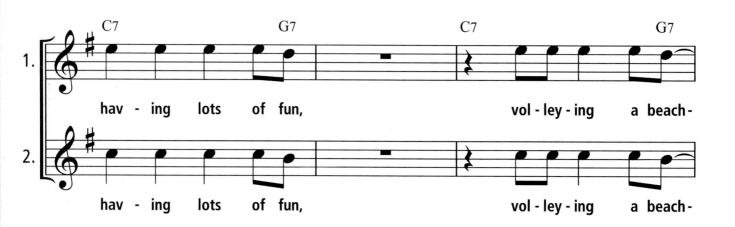

1. hav - ing lots of fun, vol - ley - ing a beach -

2. hav - ing lots of fun, vol - ley - ing a beach -

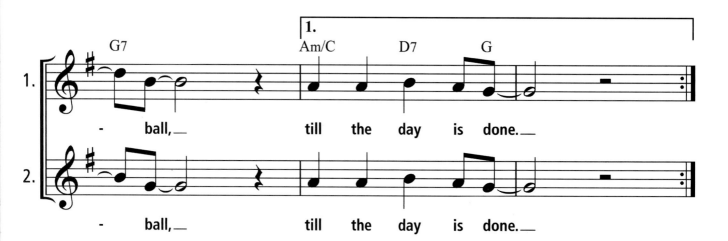

1. - ball, _ till the day is done. _

2. - ball, _ till the day is done. _

Soakin' Up the Sunshine

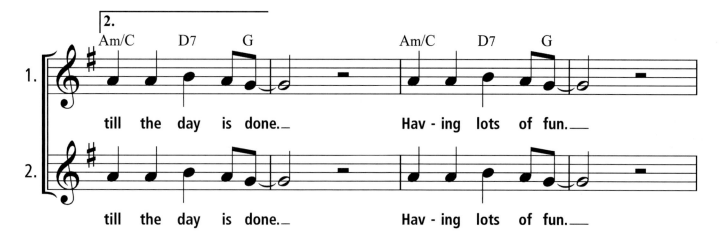

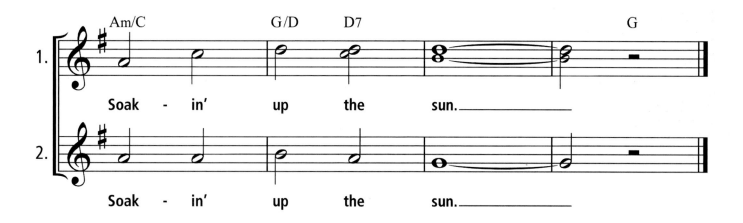

Social Studies

Words and Music by Carmino Ravosa

Social Studies

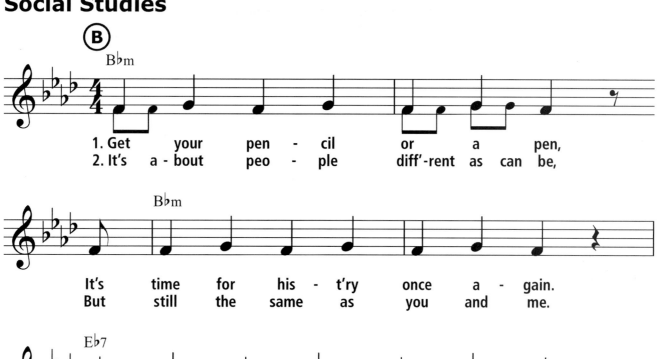

1. Get your pen - cil or a pen,
2. It's a - bout peo - ple diff'-rent as can be,

It's time for his - t'ry once a - gain.
But still the same as once you and me.

Time to o - pen up your book,
It's a - bout peo - ple true and real

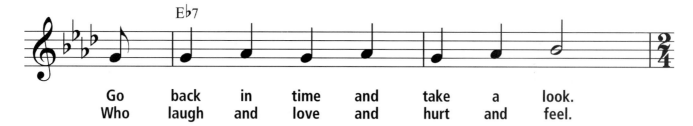

Go back in time and take a look.
Who laugh and love and hurt and feel.

4

D.C. al Coda

$\oplus$ *Coda*

2

So - cial stud - ies, so - cial stud - ies

So - cial stud - ies!

Song of the Fishes

Sea Shanty from the United States

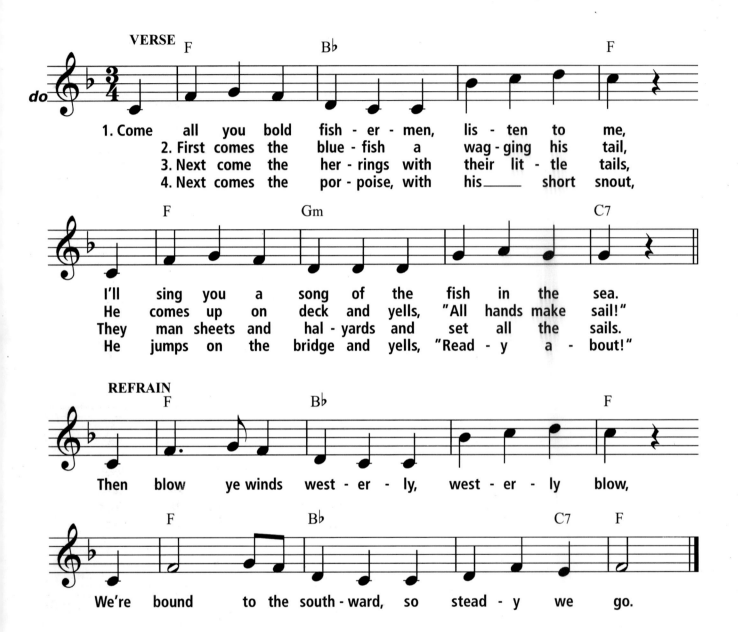

VERSE

1. Come all you bold fish - er - men, lis - ten to me,
2. First comes the blue - fish a wag - ging his tail,
3. Next come the her - rings with their lit - tle tails,
4. Next comes the por - poise, with his____ short snout,

I'll sing you a song of the fish in the sea.
He comes up on deck and yells, "All hands make sail!"
They man sheets and hal - yards and set all the sails.
He jumps on the bridge and yells, "Read - y a - bout!"

REFRAIN

Then blow ye winds west - er - ly, west - er - ly blow,

We're bound to the south - ward, so stead - y we go.

5. Then comes the mackerel,
   with his striped back,
   He flopped on the bridge
   and yelled, "Board the main tack!"

6. Up jumps the fisherman,
   stalwart and grim,
   And with his big net
   he scooped them all in.

92

Sweet Potatoes

Creole Folk Song

mf 1. Soon as we all cook sweet po - ta - toes,
f 2. Soon as sup - per's done, Ma - ma hol - lers,
mp 3. Soon's we touch our heads to the pil - low,
mf 4. Soon's the roos - ter crow in the morn - in',

Sweet po - ta - toes,   Sweet po - ta - toes,
Ma - ma hol - lers,   Ma - ma hol - lers,
To the pil - low,   To the pil - low,
In the morn - in',   In the morn - in',

Soon as we all cook sweet po - ta - toes,
Soon as sup - per's done, Ma - ma hol - lers,
Soon's we touch our heads to the pil - low,
Soon's the roos - ter crow in the morn - in',

Eat 'em right straight up!
"Get a - long to bed!"
Go to sleep right smart!
Got - ta wash our face!

93

Take Me Out to the Ball Game

Music by Albert Von Tilzer
Words by Jack Norworth
Arranged by Robert W. Smith

That's What I Call a Friend

Words and Music by
Marti Lunn Lantz and Lois Brownsey

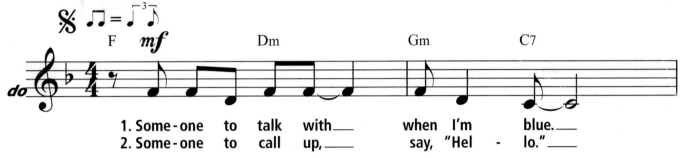

1. Some-one to talk with____ when I'm blue.____
2. Some-one to call up,____ say, "Hel - lo."____

Some-one to play with,____ that's good, too.____
Some-one to lean on,____ when you're low.____

Second time To Coda

Hang - in' to-geth - er what - ev - er we do.____
I won't for - get you, wher - ev - er I go.____

That's what I call a friend.____

That's What I Call a Friend

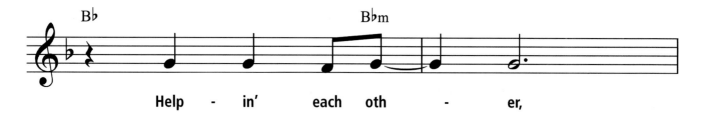

Help - in' each oth - er,

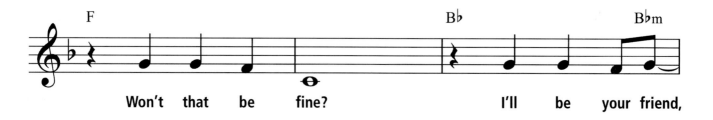

Won't that be fine? I'll be your friend,

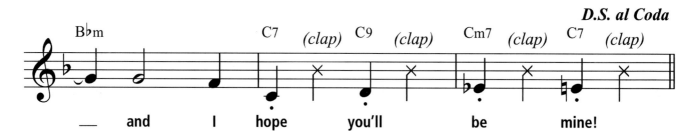

D.S. al Coda

— and I hope you'll be mine!

Coda

That's what I call a friend.___ That's what I

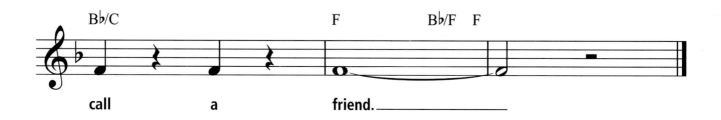

call a friend._____

There Was an Old Man

Rhythmic Setting by Konnie Saliba
Edward Lear

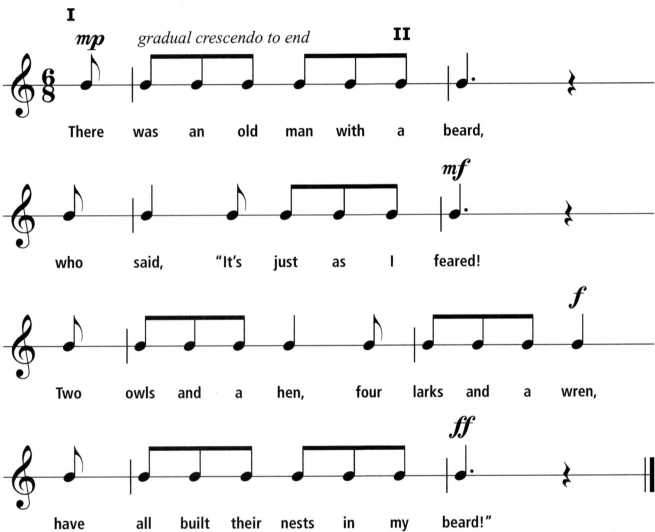

There was an old man with a beard,

who said, "It's just as I feared!

Two owls and a hen, four larks and a wren,

have all built their nests in my beard!"

This Old Man

Folk Song from England

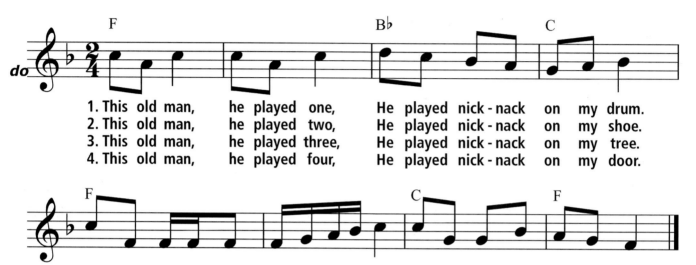

do

F

1. This old man,   he played one,   He played nick - nack   on   my drum.
2. This old man,   he played two,   He played nick - nack   on   my shoe.
3. This old man,   he played three,   He played nick - nack   on   my tree.
4. This old man,   he played four,   He played nick - nack   on   my door.

B♭   C

F   C   F

Nick - nack pad - dy - whack, give the dog a bone. This old man came roll - ing home.

5. This old man, he played five,
   He played nick-nack on my hive.

6. This old man, he played six,
   He played nick-nack on my sticks.

7. This old man, he played seven,
   He played nick-nack on my oven.

8. This old man, he played eight,
   He played nick-nack on my gate.

9. This old man, he played nine,
   He played nick-nack on my line.

10. This old man, he played ten,
    He played nick-nack on my hen.

Train Is A-Comin'

African American Spiritual

1. Train is a - com - in', oh, yes,
2. Bet - ter get your tick - et, oh, yes,
3. Room for man - y oth - ers, oh, yes,

Train is a - com - in', _____ oh, yes,
Bet - ter get your tick - et, _____ oh, yes,
Room for man - y oth - ers, _____ oh, yes,

Train is a - com - in', Train is a - com - in',
Bet - ter get your tick - et, Bet - ter get your tick - et,
Room for man - y oth - ers, Room for man - y oth - ers,

Train is a - com - in', oh, yes.
Bet - ter get your tick - et, oh, yes.
Room for man - y oth - ers, oh, yes.

The Twelve Days of Christmas

Christmas Song from England

The Twelve Days of Christmas

Walk Together, Children

African American Spiritual

1. Oh, walk to - geth - er, chil - dren,
2. Oh, talk to - geth - er, chil - dren,
3. Oh, sing to - geth - er, chil - dren,
4. Oh, shout to - geth - er, chil - dren,

Don't you get____ wear - y,

Walk to - geth - er, chil - dren,
Talk to - geth - er, chil - dren,
Sing to - geth - er, chil - dren,
Shout to - geth - er, chil - dren,

Don't you get wear - y,

Oh, walk to - geth - er, chil - dren,
Oh, talk to - geth - er, chil - dren,
Oh, sing to - geth - er, chil - dren,
Oh, shout to - geth - er, chil - dren,

Don't you get____ wear - y,

There's a great camp - meet - ing in the prom - ised land.____

You're a Grand Old Flag

Words and Music by
George M. Cohan

You're a grand old flag, you're a high - fly - ing flag;

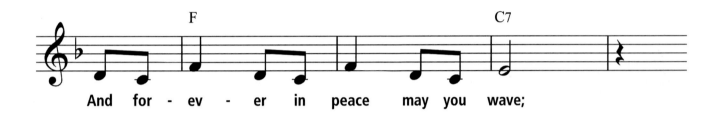

And for - ev - er in peace may you wave;

You're the em - blem of the land I love,

The home of the free and the brave.

You're a Grand Old Flag

Ev - 'ry   heart   beats   true   un - der   red,   white,   and   blue,

Where   there's   nev - er   a   boast   or   brag;

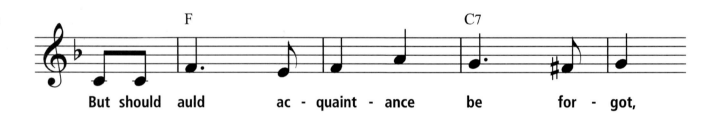

But   should   auld   ac - quaint - ance   be   for - got,

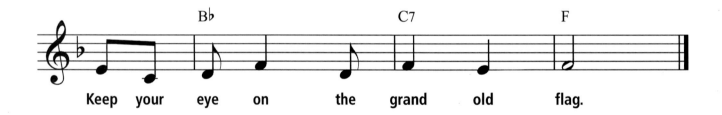

Keep   your   eye   on   the   grand   old   flag.

Zumba, zumba

Folk Song from Spain
English Words by Margaret Marks

REFRAIN

Zum - ba, zum - ba - le al pan - de - ro al pan - de - ro y al ra - bel
Zum - ba, zum - ba! Strike the cym - bal. Zum - ba, zum - ba! Strike the gong.

to - ca to - ca la zam - bom - ba da - le da - le al al - mi - rez
Zum - ba, zum - ba! Beat the tim - bal and the tam - bou - rine and drum!

Zumba, zumba

D.C. al Fine

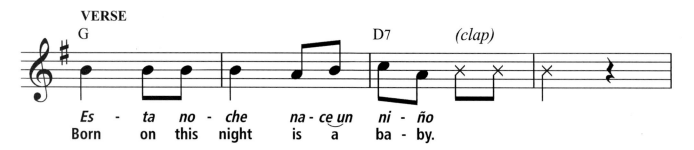

Es - ta no - che na - ce un ni - ño
Born on this night is a ba - by.

blan - co ru - bio y co - lo - ra - do
Ev - 'ry - one brings him a pres - ent,

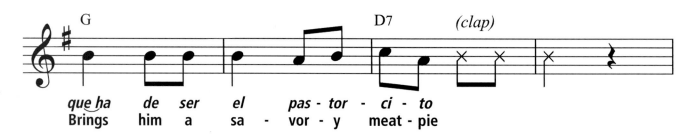

que ha de ser el pas - tor - ci - to
Brings him a sa - vor - y meat - pie

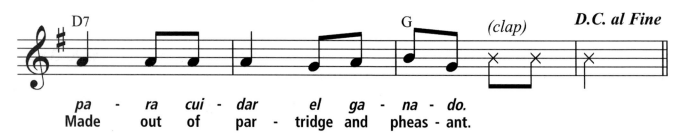

pa - ra cui - dar el ga - na - do.
Made out of par - tridge and pheas - ant.

Index